Beautiful COTSWOLDS

Stephen Dorey

Text John Mannion

MYRIAD
LONDON

Key
- Around Cheltenham and Gloucester
- Around Cirencester
- North Cotswolds
- South Cotswolds
- East Cotswolds
- Around Stroud

First published in 2008 by
Myriad Books Limited
35 Bishopsthorpe Road,
London SE26 4PA

Photographs copyright ©
Stephen Dorey
Text copyright © John Mannion

John Mannion has asserted his
right under the Copyright,
Designs and Patent Act 1998 to
be identified as the author of
this work.

ISBN 1 84746 140 9

EAN 978 1 84746 140 7

Designed by Jerry Goldie
Graphic Design

Printed in China

Map artwork by Stephen Dew

www.myriadbooks.com

CONTENTS

1 AROUND CHELTENHAM AND GLOUCESTER 6

2 AROUND CIRENCESTER 32

3 NORTH COTSWOLDS 50

4 SOUTH COTSWOLDS 74

5 EAST COTSWOLDS 90

6 AROUND STROUD 104

INTRODUCTION

I fell in love with the Cotswolds as soon as I moved from London to Gloucestershire over 30 years ago. Since then, familiarity has not bred contempt but rather a deeper affection.

When I arrived I was immediately struck by the unique beauty of the Cotswolds. Working first as a Cotswold Warden and later as a Senior Countryside Officer I was fortunate in being able to spend much of my professional life in the Gloucestershire countryside and in being able to explore much of it at first hand.

As I got to know the area better the thing that stood out most was the unity provided by the underlying oolitic limestone. The Cotswolds is an area in which humans have worked in harmony with the landscape for many hundreds of years.

The cottages, barns, churches and manor houses are all built from the local stone and are then joined together by drystone walls of the same material. Many hundreds of years ago masons found how to get the best from the stone and it has not been felt necessary to make any great changes since. In consequence, it can sometimes be difficult to accurately date a building as the architectural style and techniques have survived largely unaltered.

The protection offered by the Cotswolds' status as the country's largest Area of Outstanding Natural Beauty should help to ensure that future generations will be able to enjoy much of what we see today.

I had been trained in architectural photography and worked as a member of the Post Office Photographic Unit in London before my move, so soon after I arrived in Gloucestershire I began to build up a collection of photographs of the area. As time and commitments have allowed I've added images year by year ever since.

People sometimes ask me whether, after all this time, I haven't photographed every square inch of the Cotswolds. Far from it! I am a wanderer, and on a nice day I will set out with only a vague sense of destination. This lack of an agenda leaves me free to enjoy that sense of serendipity in discovering a lane or valley that I have not seen before. It's a world I never tire of, and I hope I never will.

Stephen Dorey

PART ONE

AROUND CHELTENHAM AND GLOUCESTER

THE WESTERN EDGE of the Cotswolds is dominated by a large escarpment – the Cotswold edge – and by the river Severn and its tributaries which flow out of the surrounding hills. The river has carved out deep and wide valleys and prosperous towns on the flood plain benefit from their shelter. The Severn estuary also gives access to the sea and Gloucester has long been a major port for the west of England. Throughout the Middle Ages the Cotswolds' wealth was built on wool, whilst its honey-coloured stone became a mainstay of local architecture.

TOWN & COUNTRY

The elegant spa town of Cheltenham retains an air of Georgian grandeur due in part to its superb Regency architecture. Crickley Hill, to the south, is on the edge of the Cotswold escarpment.

Cheltenham's history

Early settlements at Cheltenham were noted for their peacefulness and quiet prosperity but the discovery of a spring, in what is now Cheltenham Ladies' College, in 1716 gave rise to a sudden burst of popularity and affluence. During the Regency period Cheltenham Spa rivalled Bath in its splendour as the rich and the fashionable came to take the waters. Handel and Dr Samuel Johnson were among the town's notable visitors but the Spa reached the pinnacle of its success with the five-week visit of King George III in 1788. Much of the architecture and layout of today's town dates from this period. In the 19th century the passing trade of the Spa was gradually replaced by permanent residents – often, it is said, retired colonial officers suffering from liver complaints! The Regency passion for horse-racing is maintained at Cheltenham racecourse, home to the annual Cheltenham Festival and Cheltenham Gold Cup.

Cheltenham today

The town retains many of its fine Regency features such as spacious squares, crescents, terraces, promenades and beautifully laid out formal gardens. These are to be found on either side of the striking tree-lined Promenade which also contains many shops and remarkable buildings. The source of Cheltenham's wealth can be seen in its neo-classical Pittville Pump Room complete with an elegant circular bandstand. As well as horse-racing Cheltenham hosts several major festivals each year, including those devoted to music, science and literature. On a more modern note, the GCHQ building, nicknamed the Doughnut, is home to the government surveillance programme and is also located in Cheltenham. At the racecourse is the southern terminus of the Gloucestershire Warwickshire Railway, entirely run by volunteers.

Postlip Farm

The tiny hamlet of Postlip is graced with both a Jacobean manor house and a Norman chapel. The hamlet is situated at the head of the Isbourne valley where the heights of Cleeve Common dominate the landscape. The chapel retains its Norman south doorway and chancel arch and its roof dates from the 16th century. A nearby 15th century tithe barn is decorated with a stone carving on its western gable end. It is supposed to represent the 12th century Sir William de Postlip, who, according to local folklore, descends from his perch at midnight to drink from a nearby well.

Cleeve Common

Cleeve Hill and Cleeve Common form a broad expanse (about 1000 acres) of gently sloping open countryside just to the north-east of Cheltenham. Here can be found West Down which, at 1082ft (330m), is the Cotswolds' highest point. Magnificent views over the Severn Vale and the Malvern Hills are easily accessible from the scarp slope that rises out of Cheltenham. The area is popular with walkers and riders and there is plenty of wildlife to observe in addition to the more traditional Cotswold cattle and sheep. The common was an important grazing area during the Middle Ages and an earthwork known as the Ring provides evidence of Roman livestock husbandry.

Hailes

The area around Hailes gives little clue to its vibrant past. The tranquil wooded pasture land was once the site of a Cistercian abbey that came into possession of a relic of the Holy Blood of Christ during the 13th century. Authenticated by the pope, the relic drew vast numbers of pilgrims to the area and the abbey, though never large, prospered. At the Dissolution of the Monasteries the abbey was handed over to the king's agents in 1539. Local legend states that the abbey's destruction was supervised by Thomas Cromwell but it is just as likely to have fallen into disrepair when the lead was removed from its roof. All that now remains of the abbey are parts of the cloisters but the plan of the church is preserved by strategically sited trees. Nearby is a 12th century church which preserves some interesting medieval wall paintings.

Sudeley Castle

Sudeley Castle has had a rather chequered history. There was a castle on the site in Norman times but this was replaced by Sir Thomas Boteler during the Wars of the Roses. In the Tudor period the castle became the home of Katherine Parr, the last wife of Henry VIII, and in the Civil War it was Prince Rupert's headquarters. Sudeley then fell into disrepair until it was acquired by the Dent family in 1837. Extensive restorations were carried out under Lady Emma Dent. Katherine Parr had married Thomas Seymour after the death of Henry VIII but she later died in childbirth. A portrait of Katherine and a love letter written by her to Thomas Seymour are preserved at the castle and her marble tomb in the chapel was designed by Sir Gilbert Scott.

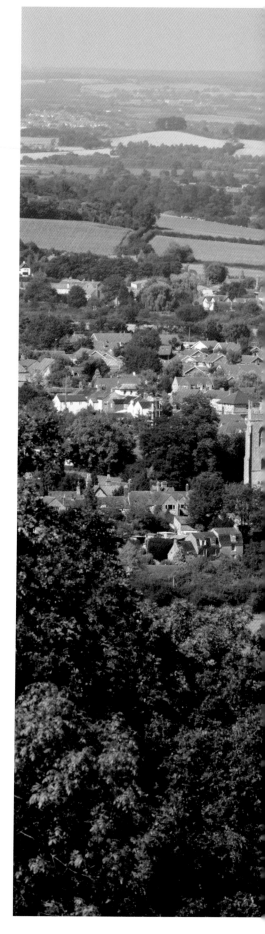

Winchcombe

The unspoilt town of Winchcombe is tucked away into the Cotswold edge and is sheltered on three sides by pleasantly wooded hills. Winchcombe was one of the seats of the Saxon kings of Mercia and was later a county town until it was absorbed by Gloucestershire. In the Middle Ages its abbey was a place of pilgrimage for followers of the martyred St Kenelm. The abbey has now completely disappeared. Most of the buildings that distinguish the town today are largely the legacy of the Cotswold wool trade. The town also benefited from its proximity to Sudeley Castle when the castle was the seat of great magnates and a host for royal visits.

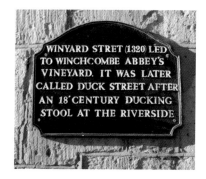

St Peter's Winchcombe

At the centre of Winchcombe is St Peter's, a justly celebrated example of a Cotswold "wool" church. The original Norman church was rebuilt in the Perpendicular style between 1460 and 1470. The west tower has three stages and is surmounted by battlements, pinnacles and gargoyles. A series of grotesque heads adorn many parts of the exterior and a gilded weathercock was added in 1874. Inside the church there is a rather sad wall-mounted memorial to Thomas Williams of Corndean, who died in 1636. It contains a single kneeling effigy of William in painted stone but the figure of his wife, who remarried after his death, was never added. Major restoration took place during the Victorian period but happily the atmosphere of the church has remained intact.

Leckhampton

Despite becoming a suburb of Cheltenham, Leckhampton has managed to maintain its own character and charm. The old village grew up around Leckhampton Court (now a Sue Ryder Hospice) and its associated church, and both buildings are still very much in evidence today. The church has an elegant tower and spire and preserves some interesting brasses and memorials. At the end of the 18th century Brandon Trye, a local landowner, developed quarries in the area and built a horse-drawn railway to transport stone into Cheltenham. One particularly hard pillar of rock was left untouched by the quarrymen and is now known as the Devil's Chimney. In the 20th century the owner of the quarries tried to fence them off and restrict access to the nearby common. This led to a riot in which eight men were arrested and sentenced to hard labour. Public access to the common was secured in 1929 when it was acquired by Cheltenham town council.

Cooper's Hill

Cooper's Hill is a spur of the Cotswolds that juts out into the Severn Vale. Now part of a 137 acre nature reserve, the lower slopes of the hill are covered in fine beech woods and the open, flower-rich upper slopes afford superb views across the valley. A large Iron Age hill fort is also part of the reserve. At the top of the hill is a maypole which forms the centrepiece of the annual cheese-rolling event. This is held every spring bank holiday Monday and participants pursue seven-pound local cheeses (strengthened with discs of wood) down a one-in-two slope. Winners are rewarded with the cheeses. Other activities on the day include uphill races. Many years ago the races were accompanied by morris dancing, wrestling matches and "girning" competitions. Girning required outstanding face-pulling abilities and, often, very few teeth. The eventual winners were presented with a horse collar.

Barrow Wake

Barrow Wake is named from the discovery of a late Iron Age burial (cAD50) which revealed three skeletons and a rich selection of grave goods including the justly famous Birdlip Mirror. Barrow Wake is also a well-known viewpoint on the Cotswold scarp that offers panoramic views of the Malvern Hills, the Severn Vale and even glimpses of Wales. The surrounding common is a site of special scientific interest in which unimproved limestone grasslands support over a hundred species of wild flowers, including some rare orchids. Twenty-two species of butterfly have been identified on the site including the comparatively rare Chalk-hill blue and the Duke of Burgundy.

Crickley Hill

Crickley Hill offers fine views across the Severn Vale and has many areas of archaeological, geological and ecological interest in its country park. Crickley Hill is the site of a hill fort that was inhabited since Neolithic times. Extensive excavations in the area have revealed that the settlement was often refortified and may even have been the site of ancient conflicts. On the Iron Age part of the site is a defensive wall standing twelve feet high but this has been reburied beneath the soil in order to preserve it. A modern visitors' centre provides information on all aspects of the area.

Gloucester

Built mainly on the eastern bank of the river Severn and dating back to Roman times, Gloucester is sheltered by the Cotswolds to the east, by the Forest of Dean to the west, while the Malvern Hills protect the city from the north-west. Gloucester's cathedral has its origins in an abbey founded in 681 and is the burial place of King Edward II. In the Middle Ages it was a centre for pilgrimage. Gloucester's long and prosperous history as a trading centre, inland port and spa can be glimpsed in the many fine buildings and churches that adorn the city.

Gloucester Docks

The docks were opened in 1827 and allowed direct access by seagoing ships to Gloucester via the Severn estuary and a ship canal. At the docks goods could be transferred to canal barges for transportation throughout the Midlands. The docks and warehouses were further expanded in 1848 to cope with increased corn imports following the repeal of the Corn Laws. By the 1980s most commercial traffic had died away and the docks now provide spacious accommodation and ample leisure facilities. The survival of the old warehouses makes the main basin a popular location for filming period drama; fans of *The Onedin Line* will find the Biddle's warehouse familiar.

Elkstone

This small village, six miles south of Cheltenham, has a fine 18th century rectory and probably one of the best-preserved Norman churches in the Cotswolds. The outside of the nave is decorated with interesting corbel figures and there is a remarkable tympanum over the south doorway. The interior features a vaulted chancel and many other well-preserved architectural details. Most of the furnishings date from the 17th century and include box pews, a pulpit, a reading desk and a communion rail.

Hilcot

Hilcot is a hidden gem of a valley which provides splendid opportunities for walking in pleasantly wooded countryside. The hamlet of Willecote is recorded in the Domesday Book and very little building seems to have taken place since. The unusual half-timbered farmhouse at Upper Hilcot provides evidence that the area was once rich in timber. Hilcot Brook runs through the valley before it joins the river Churn. There are few public footpaths but the roads are usually quiet enough for walkers and ramblers.

Withington

The manor of Withington was formerly held by the bishops of Worcester and several of its buildings date back to the 15th century. The Mill Inn lives up to its name and has the river Coln running through its gardens, although no water wheel is present. At the centre of the village is a well-preserved Norman church. The exterior has many Norman features including a solid tower and splendid south doorway but unfortunately the interior was rather over-enthusiastically cleaned up during the Victorian period. A large Roman villa once stood in the area and a mosaic pavement from it is now in the British Museum.

Charlton Abbots

The hamlet of Charlton Abbots is situated in the high country above the Isbourne valley and excellent views of the area can be gained from the village's churchyard. The church is Norman in origin but it was extensively restored in the 19th century. A short distance away there is a gabled manor house which dates from the Elizabethan and Jacobean periods. Both the rivers Isbourne and Coln have their sources in the area; the Isbourne flows north to join the Avon whilst the Coln flows south to join the Thames.

Colesbourne

In contrast to the open country of Charlton Abbots is the wooded Churn valley where the rather scattered village of Colesbourne can be found. Colesbourne Park features numerous exotic trees as a result of the enthusiasm of a 19th century squire, Henry Elwes. A keen botanist and forester, he scoured the world for specimen trees and planted many of them on his land at Colesbourne. Traditional timber from the estate provided the bowsprit and masts of the restored *SS Great Britain.* Today the park is renowned for its carpets of snowdrops, now totalling 160 varieties, on display in February. The village church has a Perpendicular tower and in the interior there is a remarkable vase-shaped 15th century stone pulpit.

Syreford

The hamlet of Syreford is about five miles south of Winchcombe and just north of Andoversford. The deeply incised river valley begins to broaden out below the village and provides an interesting range of natural habitats. At the right time of year few visitors can fail to be struck by the bright fields of poppies that flourish in the area. A Roman settlement was excavated nearby and a statuette of the god Mars recovered from the site now resides in the British Museum.

Dowdeswell

The quiet village of Dowdeswell was once the site of a skirmish in the Civil War. The parish church of St Michael is cruciform in shape and has a small stone spire. Unusually it has two 19th century galleries in the interior; one was used by the family of the parish priest and the other was for the lord of the manor. There is also an interesting 16th century brass of a priest. Dowdeswell House is the other major residence in the village. Some remains of Iron Age entrenchments are also visible in the area. Dowdeswell wood and Dowdeswell reservoir provide varied and interesting locations for walking and other activities.

Hawling

Hawling is in the high sheep country and provides walkers with many pleasant routes that offer extensive views over the surrounding area. One popular walk follows a bridleway from the village to Deadmanbury Gate on the western edge of Guiting woods. The village itself is small and quiet with a handsome Elizabethan manor house next to its church. The church was largely rebuilt in 1764 and has a Georgian pulpit and an interesting set of 17th century brass plaques. There is also a small Methodist chapel in the village which dates from 1837.

Notgrove and Turkdean

Notgrove and Turkdean are in the high wolds and benefit from large, open fields and extensive views; however, they are also exposed to cold winds from the north. Of the two villages, Notgrove is the more successful at avoiding the worst excesses of the weather. It is built around a green and has a small Norman church alongside a largely rebuilt manor house. Inside the church there is a large monument to the descendants of Dick Whittington (there is no mention of any cats however). Sherborne Brook rises in the village. Turkdean is on a hillside with the hamlet of Lower Dean in the valley below. The two Deans are connected by an impressive avenue of beech trees. The Norman church is in a large churchyard that takes shelter behind a row of chestnut trees.

Hazleton

Like Turkdean and Notgrove, Hazleton's high position gives excellent views over the surrounding countryside. Its relative isolation means that Hazleton has changed little in recent years but the ancient Salt Way used to pass through it and it prospered during the medieval period as a result of the wool trade. The parish church is a Norman foundation but its tower and windows belong to the later Perpendicular period. The south doorway and chancel arch are Norman and there is a very solid 13th century baptismal font. As in ancient times there is a great deal of foot and horse traffic around the village and excellent bridleways to Salperton in the north, Notgrove to the north-east and Turkdean to the east.

Lower Harford

The Domesday Book mentions a village called Harford but it has disappeared, probably as a result of the extension of sheep grazing during the Middle Ages. The bridge and farmhouse at Lower Harford are pleasantly situated in the Windrush valley. The area is notable for its unusual breeds of domestic animals such as Cotswold Lion sheep and longhorn cattle. If they are not visible in fields these animals can be tracked down in the nearby Cotswold Farm Park.

Aylworth

Aylworth also has its manor recorded in the Domesday Book but little remains here except for a farmhouse dating from the 17th and 18th centuries. The open valley leads down towards Naunton and joins the river Windrush at the Lower Harford bridge. The village is on the fourteen mile Windrush Way which follows the river Windrush from Winchcombe to Bourton-on-the-Water via Hawling, Aylworth and Lower Harford. More adventurous walkers can combine the Windrush Way with the Warden's Way to complete a 26 mile circular walk through a pleasing variety of habitats and landscapes.

Naunton

The village of Naunton lies in the upper Windrush valley and can often be seen in its entirety from nearby hills. The village has been a centre for sheep-rearing since it became monastic land in the Middle Ages. This long history of animal husbandry means that this part of the Windrush valley is home to flowers found only on unimproved limestone pasture. In particular cowslips can be found in the spring, whilst yellow rattle and orchids adorn the fields in summer. Naunton's other industry was the production of stone roofing slates; at one time 30,000 a week were dug from thin stone seams in nearby mines. The church has an imposing Perpendicular tower complete with pinnacles and gargoyles. Inside there is a carved 15th century stone pulpit and a font from about the same period. Naunton's dovecote, erected in 1660, incorporates four gables round a central turret.

Temple Guiting

Temple Guiting is situated on the river Windrush not far from Guiting Power. The Temple part of its name comes from the 12th century when the manor was owned by the Knights Templar. St Mary's church in Temple Guiting is built in an unusual combination of medieval and Georgian classical styles. Temple Guiting manor house was described by Pevsner as "one of the finest, if not the very best of the small Cotswold Tudor manor houses". Around Temple Guiting it should be possible to spot Cotswold Lion sheep in the fields. This large, white-faced, hornless breed was particularly prized in the Middle Ages for its long fleece, high growth rate and heavy wool clip. The wool they produced was the foundation of almost all of the wealth in the area and the landscape of the Cotswolds today is largely the result of this sheep husbandry.

Guiting Power

Guiting Power lies near the confluence of the river Windrush and one of its tributaries. Its name comes from a mixture of an Old English term *gyte*, which means an outpouring of water, and the name of the Le Poer family, the village's 13th century owners. The majority of houses in Guiting Power are clustered around a sloping village green with the war memorial at its centre.

Kineton

Between Temple Guiting and Guiting Power lies the tiny village of Kineton. It combines attractive housing, including a traditional village pub, shady woodland walks and access to the upper course of the river Windrush. There are at least three fords in the area, two of which are close to the village. The lower ford is easily negotiated but the upper one requires some caution. The nearby Cotswold Farm Park is home to many rare breeds of sheep, cattle, pigs and horses.

PART TWO

AROUND CIRENCESTER

THE OPEN LIMESTONE COUNTRYSIDE of the Cotswolds made the area attractive to Iron Age farmers as it was relatively easy to plough. In the Middle Ages improved horse plough technology made lowland areas more accessible and the Cotswolds became one of the country's prime sheep-rearing centres. English wool was a highly valued commodity and Cotswold towns and villages grew rich on its trade. The Industrial Revolution led to a decline in the fortunes of the Cotswolds that was not halted until modern times. Today's farming is a mixture of arable and cattle-rearing but it is no longer the major source of income for people who live in the Cotswolds.

RURAL RETREAT

The stone houses and barns that make up the picture postcard village of Duntisbourne Leer are clustered around a ford across the Dun. Crops ripen slowly in the Cotswolds because of the height of the land – as a well-known Gloucestershire proverb says, it's "as slow in coming as Cotswold barley".

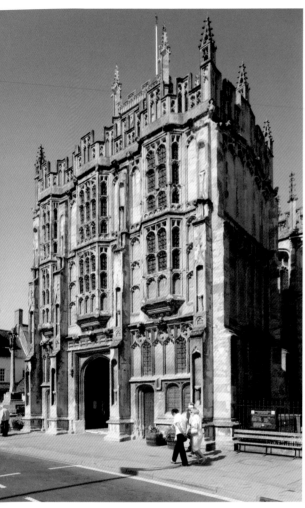

Cirencester

Cirencester was an important city during the Roman era and stood at the junction of three major roads: the Fosse Way, the Ermin Way and Akeman Street. The only visible remains of the Roman city in modern Cirencester are part of the old town wall and a large turf-covered amphitheatre. The town's prosperity in the Middle Ages was aided by the presence of a large abbey and it eventually grew to pre-eminence in the era of the wool trade. Cirencester remains a busy market town and an important crossroads in the southern Cotswolds.

Cirencester Park

Occupying some 3000 acres, Cirencester Park is laid out geometrically according to Baroque ideas about landscaping. The scheme was begun by the first Earl Bathurst in 1714-18 and is still part of the Bathurst estate. The poet Alexander Pope advised the earl and his contribution is commemorated in a small rusticated shelter known as Pope's Seat. Other features added by the earl include the hexagon, a Doric column surmounted with a statue of Queen Anne and the Gothic folly of Alfred's Hall. The park is also famous as a polo ground.

Street scenes

At the centre of Cirencester is its marketplace which even today retains a great deal of the atmosphere of a busy prosperous Cotswold wool town. Rising above the marketplace is the 162ft (49m) high Perpendicular tower of its parish church – the largest in Gloucestershire. The church once belonged to Cirencester abbey and after the Dissolution of the Monasteries it served as the town hall. The monks added the magnificent three-storey porch to the church at the end of the 15th century.

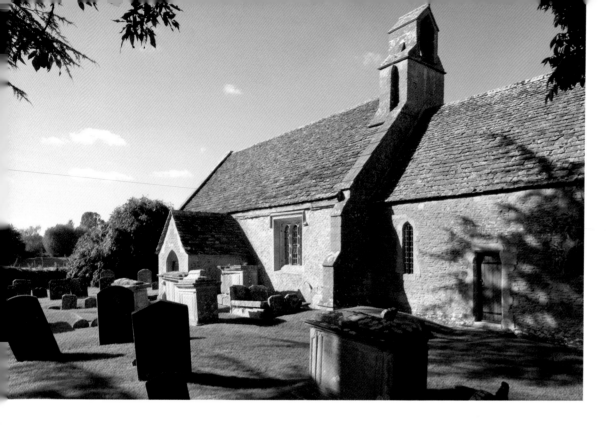

The Ampneys

This small group of villages is found, as their name suggests, on the Ampney Brook. Each has its own church and they must all have been thriving communities during the Middle Ages. The original parish of Ampney St Mary has disappeared making its church seem isolated. The present Ampney St Mary was formerly known as the hamlet of Ashbrook. The church of St Mary is a small Norman structure that still preserves many fascinating original features such as a carved lintel and medieval wall paintings. The church of the Holy Rood (an Anglo-Saxon word for cross) gives Ampney Crucis its name and there is a rare 15th century cross in its grounds. This was hidden from 17th century Puritans by being walled up inside the building. The third village in the group is Ampney St Peter. Its church is mostly Saxon in design with some Victorian additions and there is a carved pre-Christian fertility symbol in the grounds. The largest house in the area is Ampney Park which was originally constructed for the Pleydell family in 1561; its extremely well-preserved Jacobean ceiling is particularly noteworthy.

Down Ampney

Down Ampney is the birthplace of the composer Ralph Vaughan Williams. Son of the vicar, he was born in 1872 and lived in what is now the old vicarage for the first three years of his life. He composed the hymn tune *Down Ampney* to commemorate his time there.

Barnsley

Barnsley village is chiefly noted for Barnsley House Garden. Barnsley House itself dates from 1697 when it was built for a local landowner, Brereton Bouchier. It later became a parsonage but came to fame when Rosemary Verey took over its gardens in the 1950s. She created a variety of garden types including an 18th century herb garden, a knot garden, a laburnum walk, a temple with pool and a vegetable garden.

Bibury

Bibury dates back to Saxon times but the bulk of the village owes its existence to the 17th century wool trade. Arlington Row is a terrace of weavers' cottages that used to house workers from Arlington. Rack Isle, in front of the cottages and now a nature reserve, was originally used for drying wool. Alongside the traditional wool bale tombs in Bibury churchyard can be found Bisley Piece, a reminder of the 14th century when the people of Bisley angered a pope. Forbidden to bury their dead in their own churchyard they had to travel 15 miles to use this tiny graveyard at Bibury.

Coln St Dennis

Coln St Dennis enjoys a pleasant, out of the way location and its most significant building, the parish church of St James the Great, seems to have escaped the attentions of both Puritan vandals and over-enthusiastic Victorian improvers. This Norman church has an unaltered ground plan of nave, chancel and central tower. The tower is over 850 years old. An upper stage was added in the 15th century causing some stress to the pre-existing building. The church is decorated with an unusual collection of corbel figures and its interior has some interesting 18th century wall monuments.

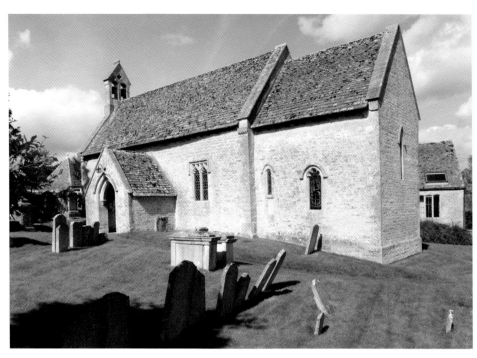

Winson

The 49 houses that make up the village of Winson are situated to the west of the river Coln. There are many pleasant walks in the vicinity, either up the Coln valley to Coln Rogers or Coln St Dennis or down it to Ablington and Bibury. More adventurous walkers can head south over the wolds to Barnsley via Barnsley Park. In spite of its size the village possesses an imposing 18th century manor house as well as a small church. The church is largely Norman but there are some 15th century additions and Victorian improvements.

Chedworth

Chedworth combines sites of both ancient and modern interest. Opposite the ancient Seven Tuns Inn a spring emerges from a wall whilst elsewhere in the village there is a sculpture of the Virgin and Child carved by Helen Rock in 1911. The church retains some Norman features but it has been sensitively added to over the centuries.
Not far from the village is Chedworth Roman villa. Discovered in 1864 and dating from AD120-400, the beautifully preserved remains include mosaic pavements (one depicting the four seasons), bath suites and a hypocaust. There is a small museum near the site.

Fossebridge

Fossebridge is where the ancient Roman Fosse Way crosses the river Coln. The 182 mile (293km) long Fosse Way originally ran between Lincoln and Exeter and was built mostly for military purposes. Today the way is little more than a track, although several major roads closely follow its route. At Fossebridge the way drops into the steep-sided Coln valley and for around 300 years there has been an inn beside the bridge to provide rest and sustenance for travellers. The present building dates largely from the 18th century and a hostelry has been recorded on the site since 1759.

Yanworth

Not far from the Chedworth Roman villa is the delightful village of Yanworth. Its Norman church stands slightly outside the village amongst a group of farm buildings. The church is chiefly remarkable for its 16th century wall painting of a scythe-bearing Father Time. The village is on the Macmillan Way and makes a good starting point for walks to Chedworth to the south-west or Hampnett to the north-east.

Stowell

Stowell is the site of a large Elizabethan mansion set in extensive parklands that command views over the Coln valley to the west. The mansion is not open to the public, but beside it there is a small Norman church that is well worth a visit. The exterior has been extensively restored but the interior contains some very early apocalyptic paintings, which are thought to have been produced soon after the church was constructed between 1150-1200. The church lies within the bounds of the estate and has to be approached on foot, but the pleasant grounds make the walk worthwhile.

Northleach

Northleach was one of the most important Cotswold wool towns in the Middle Ages and its heyday as a medieval trading centre can still be glimpsed in its market square and many half-timbered buildings. The most obvious legacy of Northleach's pre-eminence in the wool trade is its church. This was largely rebuilt in the Perpendicular style in the 15th century and is a magnificent example of the style and period. The pinnacled south porch is said to be without equal in England and the tower combines both elegance and strength. The generous windows in the clerestory provide ample light for such features as a 15th century goblet-shaped pulpit and a new ceiling designed by Sir Basil Spence. The church also has an extensive collection of brasses which commemorate the wool merchants whose wealth made the rebuilding and remodelling of the church possible.

Northleach history

Elsewhere in Northleach there are many other examples of civic pride and benefaction. These include: a free grammar school founded in 1558; two sets of almshouses, one of which was exclusively for women; and a late 18th century house of correction. This prison was built by local philanthropist Sir William Blackburn under the direction of the prison reformer Sir Onesiphorus Paul. It can be found at the crossing of the Fosse Way just to the west of the main town. In the 18th century Northleach benefited greatly from being on a coaching route between London, Oxford, Gloucester and South Wales. It is said that Thomas Telford deliberately diverted the route through the town. Northleach did not have a sufficient water supply to take advantage of the Industrial Revolution and it went into serious decline during the early 19th century. In 1831 there were only 126 occupied houses and 795 inhabitants. It is hard to imagine such a

dismal prospect in today's Northleach with its prosperous High Street and well-tended buildings. An unusual attraction is the *World of Mechanical Music*, a museum of music boxes, mechanical instruments and automatons.

Farmington

The village of Farmington stands on high ground between the valleys of the river Leach and the Sherborne Brook. Approaching it on foot can be challenging but worthwhile. The principal house in the village is Farmington Lodge. This is a mixture of 18th and 19th century styles and is fronted by four sizeable Doric columns. A rather more graceful aspect of the village green is an octagonal pumphouse topped by an elegant cupola. This was restored and refurbished by the citizens of Farmington, Connecticut in 1931 to commemorate a long-standing connection between the two communities – a Farmington man is said to have fought at the Battle of Bunker Hill. The church is Norman in origin and still retains many Norman features such as its south doorway and chancel arch. The Perpendicular tower was added in the 15th century but is well integrated with the earlier buildings. A long barrow to the east of Farmington is at least 4000 years old whilst to the west Norbury Camp has provided both Iron and Stone Age remains.

Rendcomb

Rendcomb is an estate village which used to serve Rendcomb Court, an Italianate mansion built during the 19th century by Thomas Cubitt. Since 1920 it has been a boarding school catering for pupils from the ages of three to 18. The parish church of St Peter dates largely from the 14th century but its chief glory is a carved 12th century font. The font was created between 1130-40 and shows images of the 12 Apostles; 11 are identifiable by symbols but the twelfth, representing Judas, is blank with only a pair of feet showing. Only Hereford cathedral can boast a comparable font. The 15th century rood screen was rebuilt and reassembled during the Victorian period; the original wood was re-used with cast-iron as reinforcement for the older material. Pleasant walks in the area can be achieved by following the Churn south to North Cerney and Baunton or south-west to Woodmancote and Duntisbourne Rouse.

Hampnett

The village of Hampnett centres on a large village green and is close to the source of the river Leach. Its parish church of St George is largely Norman but during the 1880s its interior was decorated with extensive stencil work. It could be argued that such designs obscure the clean lines of the Norman church but on the other hand, during the Norman and medieval periods, most churches would have had similarly decorated walls. Hampnett is on the Macmillan Way and has many fine walks leading from it.

Calmsden

The hamlet of Calmsden is distinguished by a rare 14th century wayside cross. Mounted on sturdy stepped stones the upright is still visible but the cross piece has disappeared. A spring emerges above ground nearby and a row of estate cottages built during the 19th century also add charm to the area. The Old House dates from the 16th century and is a classic example of Cotswold vernacular architecture. Calmsden is the starting point for many fine walks through both open and wooded countryside.

Pinbury *(far right)*

Pinbury Park consists of a large 16th century house enclosed by a wooded landscape. The house is associated with the Arts & Craft movement and features an early 20th century terraced garden. Deer can occasionally be spotted in the woods and there are splendid views overlooking the Frome valley.

North Cerney

North Cerney consists of a single street with views across the Churn valley. The church with its saddleback tower was largely rebuilt in the 1470s following a fire but it retains some Norman features. The interior is said to be one of the best furnished in England and has a finely carved stone pulpit. The churchyard contains a well-restored 14th century cross but visitors will also wish to seek out some of the unusual 16th century graffiti on the exterior wall; one carving seems to be of a mythical beast, with a lion's head and tail but the body of a man, known as a manticore. The primary school was founded in 1844 and there is also a Methodist chapel dating from 1891. The large lime tree on the village green marks the site where Methodist camp meetings took place in the 19th and early 20th centuries.

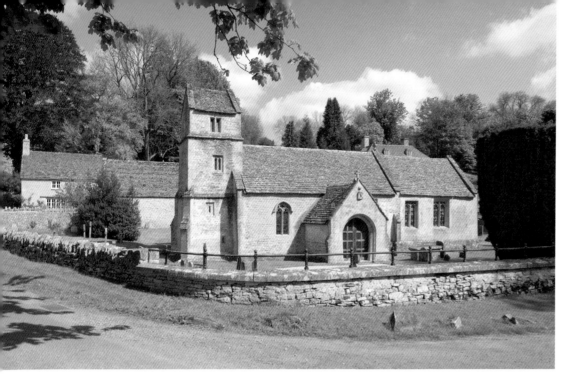

Bagendon

Bagendon is a small village situated in a quiet wooded valley. Before the Roman conquest the area known as Bagendon Dykes was the capital of the Celtic Dobunni tribe. The earthworks were excavated in the 1950s and revealed a surprisingly sophisticated pre-Roman lifestyle. Bagendon church has a saddleback tower and a chancel that is higher than the nave; this arrangement was probably made to avoid flooding.

The Duntisbournes

The four villages that bear the name Duntisbourne are strung out in a line along the Dun Brook. They are: Duntisbourne Abbots, Duntisbourne Leer, Duntisbourne Rouse and Middle Duntisbourne. Only Duntisbourne Abbots and Duntisbourne Rouse have churches. Today, Duntisbourne Leer is little more than a couple of farmhouses by a ford. The more interesting of the churches is the tiny church of Saint Michael in Duntisbourne Rouse. It has a Saxon nave and, because of the sloping ground, a small crypt chapel beneath the Norman chancel; this is unusual in such a small church.

Baunton

Baunton is situated on the river Churn. Its manor house dates from the 16th century and the original village school, which operated from 1849 until 1935, can still be seen at the Old School House. Other listed buildings in the village include Baunton mill and Downs Farmhouse. The parish church, built originally as a chapel of ease by Augustinian monks, became the parish church in 1551 following the Dissolution of the Monasteries. Its shape and character have changed little over the years and the building preserves a large 14th century wall painting of St Christopher ferrying the Christ Child across a river.

Daglingworth

Daglingworth is built along the Duntisbourne valley and is a popular starting point for short walks in the area. Some of the cottages have their own stone footbridges to allow passage across the brook. The church stands above the rest of the village to the south. Although it is Saxon in origin, it was extensively rebuilt in the 1840s. There remains a Saxon doorway and some striking Saxon carvings set into the walls. South of the village in the manor house grounds is a medieval dovecote which uses a revolving ladder to gain access to all of the 500 nesting holes.

49

– PART THREE –

NORTH COTSWOLDS

THE COTSWOLDS, AS WE SEE THEM TODAY, are founded on wool. Wool production in the region dates from at least the Roman period but until the Middle Ages most wool was exported as raw material for spinning and weaving to places like Ypres, Ghent and Bruges. When Cotswold communities began spinning and weaving their own cloth new wealth poured into the area. The money paid for the great houses, the massive Perpendicular churches and even the labourers' cottages that give the Cotswolds their unique character. The area remained rich until the Industrial Revolution introduced "king cotton" as the material of choice for most clothing.

COTSWOLD CROSSROADS
Regarded by many as the classic Cotswold village Broadway lies at the bottom of the steep escarpment and gained prosperity as a coaching town. At Snowshill, just above Broadway, sheep graze as they have done for centuries.

Stow-on-the-Wold

Stow-on-the-Wold has the dubious distinction of being the highest town, at 800ft (244m), in the Cotswolds. A popular rhyme begins, "Stow-on-the-Wold, where the wind blows cold", and the shape of its unusual market square is in part dictated by the need for stallholders to be protected from the wind. Despite its position, Stow-on-the-Wold has been a thriving market town since at least 1107 when it received its first royal charter. There were two annual fairs by the 15th century and Daniel Defoe reported the sale of 20,000 sheep in a single day there in the

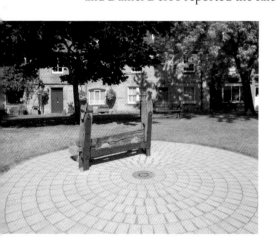

18th century. In later years Stow-on-the-Wold became famous for its horse fairs, but nowadays the only horses at the two charter fairs, one held in May and one in October, are likely to be on the merry-go-rounds. Stow-on-the Wold is also the site of one of the last major battles of the Civil war. A royalist march on Oxford with 3,000 men was thwarted by Cromwellian forces and 1,000 men were imprisoned in the church. Other disruptions to the town's peace are likely to have been dealt with in the town stocks. Originally set up in the 15th century, they have been replaced on several occasions since then.

Stow-on-the-Wold

At the centre of the town and
dominating its market square is the
parish church of St Edward which
was built between the 11th and the 15th
centuries. It was restored in the 1680s
after it had been used as a Civil War
prison and was later extensively
improved in 1847. Its tower, completed
in 1447, is 88ft (27m) high and houses
the heaviest peal of bells in
Gloucestershire. The current church
clock was made in 1926 but there have
been clocks on the tower since 1580.
In the market square there is a
medieval cross although its headstone
was replaced in 1878. The bustling
medieval horse fair has now been
relocated from the marketplace and
a more modern version is held every
May and October in a field towards
the village of Maugersbury.

Upper Slaughter

Although it sounds bloodthirsty, the name Slaughter is probably derived from the Old English word *slohtre* meaning slough or boggy place. The two villages that bear the name are both beautifully situated on the upper reaches of the river Eye. They are only half a mile away from each other, but they are very different in character. Upper Slaughter consists of cottages grouped around a small square with a church alongside; the cottages were reconstructed by Sir Edwin Lutyens in 1906. In spite of its name, Upper Slaughter is a double "thankful" village: all the men it sent to fight in the First and Second World Wars returned home alive.

Lower Slaughter

At one end of Lower Slaughter is a large millpond which feeds a working water wheel. The 19th century mill – the Old Mill – with its distinctive tall redbrick chimney, is open to the public and houses a museum. The village hall was built in 1887 and provides a late Victorian attempt at a traditional Cotswold style. Also dating from the 19th century is St Mary's church which was rebuilt in 1867. It has an imposing spire but there is little else of interest in the building apart from some 13th century arches from the original church between the nave and south aisle.

Lower Slaughter

Lower Slaughter manor house dates back to 1650 when it was built for Valentine Strong, the owner of a quarry at Little Barrington. The house has been remodelled since its construction but its grounds preserve one of the largest dovecotes in Gloucestershire. Several simply built footbridges span the river Eye in Lower Slaughter and another links the village with Upper Slaughter. The two villages can easily be explored together. Lower Slaughter tends to be more photogenic and attracts more visitors than its neighbour but Upper Slaughter is not without its charms.

Longborough

Longborough is pleasantly situated on a hillside overlooking the Evenlode valley. The village church has a 13th century tower with an added 15th century upper section in the Perpendicular style. The windows of the south porch are in the Decorated style characteristic of the 14th century.

Donnington

Close to Stow-on-the-Wold is the hamlet of Donnington. It was here that the royalist Lord Astley surrendered after the Battle of Stow, one of the final actions of the Civil War. The hamlet gives its name to the nearby Donnington Brewery which supplies many Cotswold inns and pubs. The brewery has a working water-powered mill wheel.

Lower Oddington

Lower and Upper Oddington form a single community on the slopes of a hill between Stow-on-the-Wold and the river Evenlode. Just south of the village is the church of St Nicholas. This dates from the 13th and 14th centuries and because of its relative isolation it largely escaped misguided attempts to improve it. The most striking feature of the interior is the extensive 14th century wall painting showing the Last Judgement and the torment of the damned. Created around 1340, the Doom painting occupies the entire north-west wall of the church. "Doom" paintings, designed to portray religious ideas to a largely illiterate population, were common features of medieval churches.

Upper and Lower Swell

Upper and Lower Swell are associated with the river Dikler that rises nearby. At Upper Swell there is a small 18th century bridge and beyond it a moss-covered weir which holds back an extensive millpond. The attached mill still has its water wheel. Further into the village there is a 16th century manor house. Lower Swell has another bridge at its eastern end and features some fine buildings. The church lies between the two villages. The original Norman building now forms its south side. Nearby are Abbotswood Gardens which were designed by the renowned architect Sir Edwin Lutyens. The gardens are often open to the public under the National Gardens Scheme.

Moreton-in-Marsh

Moreton-in-Marsh straddles the Fosse Way and its position on various transportation routes accounts for its existence and prosperity. During the 17th and 18th centuries it was on the main coaching route between London, Oxford, Worcester and Hereford. When coaching declined the town quickly moved on to railways; the Stratford-Moreton tramway opened in 1826 and was one of the earliest railways in the country. A mainline service arrived in 1843 and the line between London, Oxford and Worcester was opened in 1853. As a centre for travellers Moreton-in-Marsh is well provided with inns one of which, the 16th century White Hart (Royal) Hotel, was used by Charles I during the Civil War. It is also said to be haunted. The Curfew Tower on the corner of Oxford Street still has its original 1633 curfew bell hanging in it. The bell was in daily use until 1860 and even occasionally afterwards for summoning the fire brigade. Chastleton House, three miles south-east of the town, is a fine Jacobean manor house which still contains much of its original furniture; it is now run by the National Trust.

Two miles from Moreton-in-Marsh is the Four Shires Stone, a Cotswold stone pillar that marked the coming together of the four counties of Gloucestershire, Worcestershire, Oxfordshire and Warwickshire. Unfortunately county boundary changes have left the stone out of date.

Moreton-in-Marsh market

Hand-in-hand with travel comes trade and Moreton has been a market centre for centuries. The first charter for a weekly market was granted to Moreton-in-Marsh in 1227 and in 1267 the town was granted a fair. A new charter was granted by Charles I in 1638. The ability to hold a market meant that the town benefited greatly from the influx of people but also that the town authorities could charge tolls and levies in return for services such as law enforcement. The administrative centre for such activities was usually a market hall. The neo-Tudor style Redesdale market hall in Moreton-in-Marsh was built in 1887 and was designed by Sir Ernest George. More permanent trade was centred on the High Street with its stone-built shops, houses and coaching inns.

Bourton-on-the-Hill

Visitors to the Cotswolds might be forgiven for thinking that previous generations did not give a great deal of thought to the naming of places. There are four Duntisbournes, three Ampneys and a profusion of places with Upper and Lower versions. Stow-on-the-Wold in Old English just means place on a hill. Bourton-on-the Hill is near Bourton Downs but confusingly it is about 10 miles from Bourton-on-the-Water. The village of Bourton-on-the-Hill was once owned by the abbots of Westminster who also had large sheep runs on the nearby downs. The wealth created by the 15th century wool industry enabled the building of a particularly fine clerestory on the church. The three-stage tower also dates from the Perpendicular period but the weighty arched columns of the interior reveal its Norman origins. The church also preserves a bell metal bushel and peck from 1816. These standard measures were once required by law in every church so that they could be used for the gathering of tithes and for settling disputes. At the top of the hill is a substantial 18th century coaching inn. The village also contains many fine 17th and 18th century cottages.

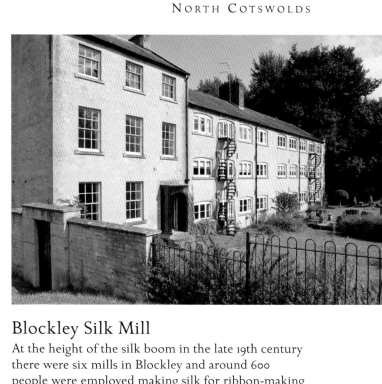

Blockley Silk Mill

At the height of the silk boom in the late 19th century there were six mills in Blockley and around 600 people were employed making silk for ribbon-making factories in Coventry. The old silk mill can still be seen beyond a pool near the church; the other mills are now substantial private dwellings. Many of the terraced cottages on the northern edge of the village were once occupied by silk weavers.

Blockley

Blockley was one of the first villages in England to produce its own electricity, thanks to the power of the Blockley Brook. In previous centuries the brook provided the energy for corn mills, silk throwers and even wood saws. Six mills once operated in the village although only one is still open; the beautiful Mill Dene garden has been created around another one. Parts of the church date from the Norman period but the tower was only added in 1725 by a local quarry owner Thomas Woodward. Inside the church is a series of handsome monuments to local landowners and some interesting brass monuments dedicated to former parish priests.

Ebrington

This pleasant village overlooks a valley watered by the Knee Brook as it makes its way to the river Stour. Ebrington Manor has been occupied continuously by the Fortescue family since 1456. The manor house has undergone successive renovations since the 15th century and its exterior is largely the result of 17th century alterations. Sharing a ridge above the village with the manor house is the church of St Eadburgha. It has some Norman features, such as a geometric design on the tympanum, and some medieval ones including a roundel window depicting the month of October. One of the monuments in the church is dedicated to William Kyte Esq and records his gift, in 1632, of "the milk of ten good and sufficient milch kine" to be distributed to the poor of Ebrington "from May 10th to November 1st in perpetuity".

Hidcote

The tiny hamlet of Hidcote Bartrim is famous for the National Trust owned gardens of Hidcote Manor. The 17th century Hidcote Manor was acquired in 1907 by the family of Major Lawrence Johnston. At that time its gardens consisted of little more than a few fields but once Johnston became interested they quickly grew in both size and scope so that by the 1920s Johnston employed 12 full-time gardeners. Rather than laying out a single garden Johnston laid out a series of them separated by walls and trees. He was also prepared to scour the world for exotic plants and either led or sponsored plant-collecting expeditions to the Swiss Alps, the Andes, Burma, Kenya and many other places. After devoting more than 40 years to his passion Major Johnston donated the gardens to the National Trust in 1948. The highlights of today's gardens include the White Garden, the Bathing Pool Garden and the Fuchsia Garden but the site also contains wild gardens, a kitchen garden, grass walks and a theatre lawn where an open-air production of Shakespeare takes place each summer.

Chipping Campden

The word "chipping" relates to an Old English word meaning market and it was as a wool and cattle market that the village first grew up. The many fine houses in the town are evidence of its successful trading past.

Grevel House was built for William Grevel in about 1380 and features striking Perpendicular-style two storey windows. The market hall was built in 1627 and was intended for the sale of cheese, butter and poultry in a period when the wool trade was in decline. The row of almshouses just below St James' church dates from 1612; they originally cost £1,000 and are still used today to house 12 Campden pensioners. Next to the church are the lodges and gateway to Campden House. These are some of the only remains of the original buildings as the rest were burned down during the Civil War. St James' church is a significant local landmark. It is built in the Perpendicular style and features a 15th century pinnacled tower. Its interior houses some interesting marble monuments, several monumental brasses and an excellent collection of English medieval embroidery. In the early 20th century Chipping Campden became a different kind of centre of excellence when Charles Ashbee moved his Guild and School of Handicraft to the village from London.

Chipping Campden buildings

Chipping Campden's architecture may not please purists but its growth and development over hundreds of years makes it a delight to the eye. In the gently curving High Street newer buildings were simply grafted on to older ones so that no two buildings are exactly the same and medieval buildings co-exist with houses in the Classical style. What gives the town its sense of unity is the consistent use of golden Cotswold limestone whether in the sturdy arches of the market hall or in the lofty Perpendicular pinnacles of the church.

Silk Mill

The old silk mill in Sheep Street is where CR Ashbee set up his Guild of Handicrafts in 1902. This involved moving 50 craftsmen and their families from the East End of London to Chipping Campden and setting them to work on traditional trades. Sadly this brave social experiment did not survive the rigours of the First World War and the Depression. Ashbee's workshop is now a small museum. One surviving remnant of the Guild is Harts Gold and Silversmiths.

Dover's Hill

Dover's Hill is now the site of a crescent-shaped field walk along the edge of the Cotswold escarpment, owned and managed by the National Trust. In earlier times the "Cotswold Olympicks" were held on Dover's Hill. These games started in 1612 and were held on the Thursday and Friday after Whit Sunday. Traditional activities included horse-racing and hare-coursing but the rather more violent sports of single stick fighting and shin kicking were the main attractions. Single stick fighting consisted of opponents beating each other with a stick whilst they had one hand tied behind their backs. The games fell into disrepute and were discontinued in 1853.

Saintbury

This small village is ranged along the side of Saintbury Hill. The name Saintbury probably refers to a Saxon holy man called Cada who built a small cell nearby. The Norman church still preserves some fragments of a former Saxon building. The village itself features a fine cross which stands at the crossroads to the north of the village. The lower part dates from the 15th century whilst the Maltese cross and sundial were added in 1848.

Willersey

With its pretty green, duck pond and ancient church, Willersey is a picture-book English village. The village is on the edge of the Cotswolds but its mellow-stoned, well-proportioned houses link it firmly with many of the settlements of the high wolds. In the Middle Ages the abbots of Evesham had a summer residence in Willersey and later William Roper, the son-in-law of Sir Thomas More, owned the manor. King Charles II gave the Penderel family a house here in thanks for their help in his escape after the Battle of Worcester. Most of the houses in the village date from this period or later, although the church dates largely from the 14th century.

Broadway

Regarded by many as the finest large village in the Cotswolds, Broadway, as its name suggests, has a wide main street and the village was once an important staging post on the London to Worcester route. A new turnpike road was opened in 1736 and at one time seven coaches passed through the village each day. Many of the fine buildings along Broadway's main street began their lives as inns to serve the passing trade. With the coming of the railways the coach trade died away but Broadway had its own station and it quickly became a stopping off point for exploration of the Cotswolds.

This beautifully painted house in Broadway is almost engulfed by the mature foliage adorning its front wall.

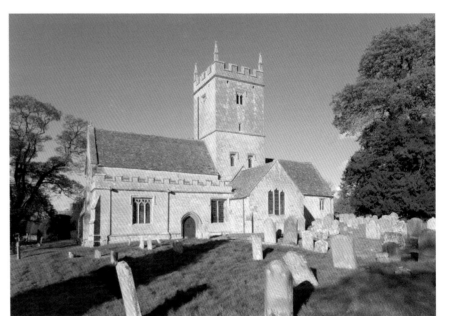

Broadway Tower

Broadway Tower is built on the site of an ancient beacon and is said to have inspired JRR Tolkien to create the tower of Amon Hen and the Hill of Seeing in *The Lord of the Rings*. The tower is certainly one of the country's premier viewpoints; on a clear day it is possible to see 13 counties and enjoy views of the Vale of Evesham, the Vale of Gloucester, the Severn valley and the Welsh mountains. The tower has also had some interesting inhabitants and owners including William Morris and the archaeologist Sir Arthur Evans; at one time it was virtually a country retreat for the pre-Raphaelites.

St Eadburgha's Church

The font and pillars of Broadway's "old" church are Norman but its dedication to the Saxon St Eadburgha suggests that it is built on the site of an earlier church. The building is delightfully situated beside a quiet lane and there is a stream at the bottom of the churchyard. It is cruciform in shape and has a largely unspoilt interior. It is now only open during the summer months.

Stanton

Stanton is essentially a single street village and is claimed by many to be one of the oldest in the Cotswolds. Most of the houses date from the 17th century but the village was extensively restored by the architect Sir Philip Stott after he purchased large tracts of it just before the First World War. Stott modernised many features but set up covenants to prevent the worst excesses of the 20th century from taking hold in the village. His work means that Stanton often provides a backdrop for period film and television shoots. Parts of Stanton's church date back to the 12th century and it features both a 14th century and a Jacobean pulpit. It has an elegant spire and some of its windows are from the 15th century.

Laverton

Laverton is a large hamlet located beneath the Cotswold edge. It contains several substantial and well-built farmhouses that date back to the 16th century and make good use of local stone. Laverton is close to the Cotswold Way and the many fine views in the area make it popular with walkers. Broadway to the north and Stanton to the south are within easy reach.

Stanway

The village of Stanway is dominated by the gatehouse to Stanway House where a mixture of Gothic, Renaissance and Dutch styles are given a pleasing unity by the local stone. Stanway House was built during the 1580s on the site of an earlier manor house. It is mostly Jacobean in style and has a remarkable 60-pane oriel window. The grounds contain a restored water garden which features the highest fountain in England, an impressive tithe barn dating from 1370 and a log-fired brewing house. The church of St Peter retains its Jacobean pulpit but elsewhere has suffered badly at the hands of Victorian restorers. Opposite the driveway to Stanway House is a thatched cricket pavilion mounted on saddle stones. This unusual building was a gift to the village by the author of *Peter Pan*, J M Barrie, who was a frequent visitor to the area in the early years of the 20th century.

Snowshill

There have been settlements near Snowshill since the Bronze Age. A barrow nearby contained a famous collection of weapons now in the British Museum. Snowshill was owned by Winchcombe abbey from 821 until the Dissolution of the Monasteries when it was given to King Henry VIII's wife Katherine Parr. The main part of the current Snowshill manor house dates from around 1500. In 1919 the almost derelict building was bought and restored by Charles Paget Wade, who needed somewhere to present his collection of 22,000 examples of craftsmanship. Amassed between 1900 and 1951 the collection is extremely diverse and illustrates Wade's idea that each object embodies the spirit of the craftsman who made it and the age in which it was produced. The collection includes automatons, butter stamps, bicycles, children's toys, clocks, cowbells, locks and 26 suits of Samurai armour.

Cutsdean

Cutsdean lies at a height of 750ft (229m) and is situated on the western slope of a Cotswold hillside. By a curiosity of administration it belonged to Worcestershire for over a thousand years and only officially became part of Gloucestershire in 1931. The church of St James is situated next to a farmyard and was rebuilt in 1863, but the tower is 14th century. The ancient trackway known as Buckle Street passes just to the west of the village, while the source of the beautiful river Windrush lies just to the north. At Cutsdean the infant river was used for the annual process of washing the sheep prior to shearing. The village's stone-lined sheep wash was recently restored by voluntary Cotswold wardens. This open rolling landscape is typical of the high Cotswolds which originally would have been vast sheep walks before being divided up by dry stone walls at the time of the enclosures.

PART FOUR

SOUTH COTSWOLDS

✧

THE COTSWOLDS HAVE ENJOYED PROSPERITY for at least 600 years. The area experienced a boom in the Middle Ages, literally off the backs of sheep, and many towns in and around the Cotswolds prospered greatly as a result of quarrying, transport or tourism. This means that the visitor can find a great deal of fine architecture in a variety of different styles from many historic periods in one relatively small area. Whether you have a taste for Classical, Perpendicular or Gothic architecture there will be something of interest in the Cotswolds and almost all of it in Cotswold stone.

COTSWOLD GRANDEUR
The beautiful village of Castle Combe on the edge of By Brook is much loved by film-makers and photographers. To the south-west, the city of Bath is famous for its splendid Georgian architecture including the Royal Crescent (right)

Bath

Bath is a city that has had two major heydays. The first was during the Roman occupation when the town of Aqua Sulis grew up around the natural hot springs in the area and the second was during the Regency and Georgian periods when the craze for taking the waters made Bath the centre of fashion and one of the largest cities in England. Substantial traces of both periods can still be seen in the city today. The city is on the very edge of the Cotswold hills and the stone in this area is usually described as creamy rather than golden. The Roman temple and baths, the abbey and the city's famous crescents are all built from locally quarried limestone. Apart from the Roman baths and the temple, the ancient city of Bath largely disappeared during the Saxon period and the city was largely in royal and monastic hands throughout the Middle Ages. The spa trade began to revive after the Dissolution of the Monasteries but

The pretty shop housing Sally Lunn's tea room is the oldest house in Bath and dates from around 1482.

it was not until after the Civil War that Bath began to be a health centre for the aristocracy. The new Bath was largely built in the Classical style with long stretches of identical façades to give impressions of palatial scale and classical decorum.

Cold Ashton Manor

Cold Ashton is situated on the southern edge of the Cotswolds and, given the literalism of much of the naming in the area, it probably derives its name from the cold winds that sweep in over the Bristol Channel. However, most people would probably be happy to tolerate the chilly location for the splendid views that its elevation affords. Cold Ashton

Manor is a large gabled building dating from the Jacobean period. It was probably erected by John Gunning, a former mayor of Bristol, in 1629. The Renaissance archway leading onto the road has square Roman Doric columns with a rosette frieze. These are surmounted by two flower-filled urns with semi-circular steps leading down from it.

Marshfield

Marshfield is another literally named town, although this may not be obvious to modern ears; it simply means a field on the march, or edge. The tower of the parish church dominates the skyline for several miles around and provides a reference point for walkers. An original Norman building was rebuilt in the Perpendicular style in about 1470. Further restorations took place in the late 19th and early 20th centuries. The town contains a splendid mixture of building styles ranging from a Georgian-Gothic tollhouse through to a medieval barn and dovecote to an early Georgian stable range.

Marshfield

Marshfield benefits from its proximity to Bath and Bristol and has been a market town since 1234. In the Middle Ages Marshfield was one of the largest towns in the area and its prosperity continued well into the 18th century. By then it was particularly concerned with the malt trade as can be seen in the many malt houses and long storage buildings at the back of some properties. Of the listed buildings in the town the almshouses established by the Crispe family between 1612 and 1619 are particularly interesting. The eight gabled houses are arranged on either side of a chapel which has a small spire and front porch. Originally each house consisted of a single room with a stone spiral staircase in one corner leading to a bedroom.

Castle Combe

Although it is well to the south of the traditional Cotswold area, Castle Combe displays many of the charms of the area and is a popular destination for visitors. The village is centred on a market cross that reflects its growth through wool trading. Other marks of this once-great industry include several fine timber-framed buildings clustered around the cross and the substantial Perpendicular tower that was added to the church in 1434. The village is situated on the By Brook and there is a charming bridge that spans the stream here. The Norman castle that gives the village its name has largely disappeared but signs of it, such as the mound on which it was built, are still present.

The photogenic charm of the village has regularly attracted film-makers. In 1966 a section of the By Brook near the bridge was converted into a miniature port complete with jetty and boats for the filming of *Dr Doolittle*. More recently Robert de Niro and Sienna Miller visited the village for the making of *Stardust*. There are many fine walks in the area and the village is on the Macmillan Way long-distance footpath. Also near the village is the Castle Combe motor racing circuit which opened in 1950 on the site of a former air base.

Great and Little Badminton

Situated some 400ft (122m) up on the Cotswolds both Badminton villages enjoy extensive views across the surrounding area. Great Badminton is famous for the annual horse trials that take place at Badminton House. Great Badminton is an estate village which means that it grew up serving the needs of nearby Badminton House. The bulk of the houses in the present village date from the late 18th and early 19th centuries. Little Badminton is just to the north of Great Badminton and although its buildings are slightly scattered it has the village green as a focal point. Badminton House is the home of the Beaufort family and is a particularly fine example of the Palladian period. The game of Badminton was invented at the house and the standard size of its court was dictated by the size of the hall. The park is partly the work of Capability Brown and contains a Great Avenue that is several miles long.

Hawkesbury

The village of Hawkesbury nestles in a wooded coombe below the Cotswold scarp. It is dominated by its parish church which dates back to the 12th century and is on the site of an earlier Saxon church. It is mainly in the Perpendicular style. The promise of the exterior is not matched by the interior which was rather over-improved from 1882-85. The Old Vicarage to the east of the church is an unusual L-shape and dates from the late 15th century. It features a two

Horton

The village of Horton is situated on the edge of the Cotswolds and is chiefly noted for its manor house, Horton Court. The main building is not open to the public but its Norman hall and a detached 16th century ambulatory are well worth a visit. The ambulatory was built by William Knight, Henry VIII's envoy to the pope. Knight's familiarity with Rome no doubt inspired the medallion heads of Roman emperors which can be seen in the gardens.

storey gabled porch and a late 18th century garden building with Gothic arched windows. Outside the village on the Cotswold edge is the Somerset Monument. This was erected in 1846 to commemorate General Lord Edward Somerset who served with distinction at Waterloo and died in 1842. Somerset was the nephew of the sixth Duke of Beaufort whose family home is at nearby Badminton. The slightly tapering square tower is approximately 100ft (30m) high and is a well-known local landmark.

Westonbirt Arboretum

The Westonbirt Arboretum was started around 1829 by the Holford family but it was not until Robert Stayner Holford inherited the estate in 1839 that it began to take shape as something out of the ordinary. Holford was influenced by the picturesque style advocated by William Gilpin and planted his trees for aesthetic effect and by 1855 most of the Old Arboretum had been laid out. This

included the areas now know as the Main Drive, Specimen Avenue, Holford Ride, Morley Ride and Jackson Avenue. Today Westonbirt is one of two national arboreta maintained by the Forestry Commission. The site covers an area of 600 acres and includes an area of ancient semi-natural woodland which consists mainly of high oaks and lower hazel coppice. Some of the woodland is being restored to its natural state after being cleared around 60 years ago but other parts are being planted with new trees such as maples. It is hoped that Westonbirt will one day house the world's best collection of maples. The purpose of the national arboreta is to conserve native woodland populations and to educate and enthuse people about trees. Westonbirt Aboretum is open to the public and provides opportunities for educational visits. The Forestry Commission also uses the arboretum for higher-level research and scientific investigation into the fauna and flora of woodland areas. All this is of course very important but most people will visit Westonbirt simply to enjoy the beauty of its trees throughout the seasons.

Tetbury

Dominating Tetbury is its 17th century Market House. This imposing building is supported on three rows of pillars and has a stone roof; it used to be even higher but it was reduced by one storey in 1817. Above the roof is a fine cupola on which there is a weather vane decorated with gilded dolphins. The dolphins also appear on the town's coat of arms. Near to the Market House are the Chipping Steps, where a livestock market used to take place amongst an imposing collection of 18th and 19th century buildings. Also in this area is Gumstool Hill where the annual Woolsack Races take place every spring bank holiday Monday. This rather gruelling event involves contestants running down Gumstool Hill (one-in-four) and up again carrying a 60lb (27kg) woolsack. Teams of young men and women – the women's sacks are only 35lb (16kg) – take part in the race whilst townspeople dress up in medieval costumes. In 1633 the town was sold to four local residents who became known as the Feoffees. Along with 13 town wardens the Feoffees virtually ran Tetbury; today they confine themselves to charitable activities. St Mary's church is an imposing

building rebuilt in the Gothic style in the late 18th century; its spire is 186ft (57m) high. The interior is illuminated by graceful Perpendicular windows and features box pews, panelled galleries and two magnificent chandeliers. Tetbury's original courthouse now houses a Police Museum which tells the story of the Gloucestershire Police Constabulary since its founding in 1839. Visitors can inspect cells, the original police office and the magistrate's court. There are around 30 antiques shops in Tetbury making it an international destination for antique dealers.

Wotton-under-Edge

Wotton-under-Edge's principal buildings are laid out on a grid plan rather than being clustered around a central square or green. This arrangement may have been an early experiment in town planning as it was carried out at the behest of Jone de Somery, the lady of the manor who granted the town its charter in 1253. The town's oldest building is the timber-framed Ram Inn which is believed to date from 1350. The parish church of St Mary the Virgin was consecrated in 1283 and possesses a fine late 14th century tower. Inside the church is the Berkeley tomb, an early 15th century table tomb with life-sized brasses (reputedly the best of their kind in England) of Thomas, 10th Baron de Berkeley (1352-1417), and his wife, Margaret. One of the first grammar schools in the country was founded at Wotton by Katharine Lady Berkeley in 1384; a comprehensive school bearing her name still operates in the town. The Church Street almshouses were built in 1638. One notable resident of Wotton was Sir Isaac Pitman who lived in a house that still stands in Orchard Street. Here he invented his system of shorthand in 1837.

North Nibley

North Nibley is a small village between Wotton-under-Edge and Dursley. The last battle between private armies fought on English soil took place at Nibley Green on March 20 1469. The contestants were William, Lord Berkeley, and Thomas, Lord Lisle, and about 1,000 men were involved; Lord Berkeley emerged the victor after a very bloody skirmish. Above the village, on Nibley Knoll, stands the Tyndale Monument. Tyndale was a prominent Protestant in the time of Henry VIII and produced the first complete translation of the *New Testament* in English. He was martyred in Vilvorde, Flanders in 1536. The 111ft (34m) high Tyndale Monument was built in 1866 using stone from Hampton quarry, near Stroud. It was believed at the time that Tyndale was born in North Nibley but nearby Slimbridge also claims this honour. The tower can be climbed using an internal winding staircase and fine views are available from the upper platform. The parish church is largely Perpendicular in style but features an unusual 19th century French-Gothic chancel designed by JL Pearson, the architect of Truro cathedral.

Kingscote

Kingscote is in the high country near Dursley and features a 13th century church. One of the interesting monuments in its churchyard is an unusual triangular stone pyramid. A tablet in the church announces that it was there that Catherine Kingscote married Edward Jenner, the discoverer of vaccination. Substantial Roman buildings have been discovered at Kingscote and there are many other Roman sites nearby.

Ozleworth

Ozleworth is set in a quiet wooded valley overlooking the National Trust owned Newark Park. The group of buildings that comprise Ozleworth can be approached through Ozleworth Park. The Norman church stands in a circular churchyard which in itself is a sign of an earlier religious site, possibly a sacred grove. The church of St Nicholas has an extremely rare hexagonal central tower dating from the early 12th century combined with a nave that was added in the 1220s. The interior boasts a fine 13th century font. The stairway to the musicians' gallery fits into the thickness of the wall, an arrangement that considerably weakens its structure.

PART FIVE

EAST COTSWOLDS

✒

ALTHOUGH MUCH OF THE COTSWOLDS is a gently undulating plateau, the area is nevertheless high enough to attract rain from the prevailing westerly winds and the limestone hills act as a natural reservoir. Many streams and rivers emerge in the Cotswolds before making their way down to either the Thames or the Severn valleys. Over the years the rivers have carved out many beautiful valleys; some are steep but many are wide and sheltered. This combination of relatively gentle hills, slow-moving rivers and streams was the basis of the Cotswolds' success as an area for sheep-farming and has combined to create the superb landscape we all know today.

WATERY DELIGHTS
Both situated on the Windrush, one of the Cotswolds' most evocative rivers, the pretty towns of Bourton-on-the-Water and Sherborne have great attractions for visitors.

Burford

Burford, the eastern gateway to the Cotswolds, built its reputation on wool, quarrying and coaching. Wool was important from the 14th century onwards and the stone from quarries near the town was used in the construction of some of Britain's finest buildings, ranging from Blenheim Palace to St Paul's cathedral. Burford's heyday as a coaching town came in the 18th century when it was an important stop on routes into Oxford and London; "Burford Bait", the huge meals served by the inns, were famous in the region. Sadly, the coaching trade died away with the advent of the railways, which also bypassed the town. Burford's steep High Street with its many inns is well known but there are many other delightful buildings and features away from the main street.

The Tolsey dates from 1500 and was formerly the place where market tolls were collected; it was also the seat of the borough court. Like many market halls it features a sheltered area and, in modern times, a clock for the convenience of traders. The Tolsey is now a museum which houses many interesting artefacts from Burford's past, stretching back to the Roman era.

Amongst Burford's most interesting houses are the 17th century Great House and a row of handsome almshouses which were built in 1457 and partially rebuilt in 1828. The church is interesting both architecturally and historically. The original Norman tower is surmounted by an elegant 15th century spire and there is also a fine two-storey fan-vaulted south porch. In the interior a memorial carving includes the first representation of Amazonian Indians in England and the font preserves the autograph of a Leveller prisoner who was kept in the church during the Civil War.

Minster Lovell

Minster Lovell combines an idyllic rural setting with buildings and ruins that reflect the village's interesting and varied past. A bridge across the Windrush leads to the High Street which has a well-balanced selection of thatched cottages and other Cotswold stone houses. St Kenelm's church was built in 1431 and has an attractive vaulted ceiling underneath the central tower. Some of the stained glass may be original and there is a fine alabaster knight's tomb, probably that of William the seventh Baron of Lovell who built the church and manor house; the house dates from 1435. Colourful local legends surround the fate of the ninth Lord Lovell who fought with Richard III at Bosworth Field and became involved in the Lambert Simnel rebellion, after which he disappeared. According to these stories, building work in the early 18th century revealed an underground vault complete with skeleton. In the mid-18th century the manor was dismantled to provide stone for nearby farm buildings. Also worth noting is the round medieval dovecote.

Swinbrook

Swinbrook is an attractive village a few miles north-east of Burford. A stream flows through the village close to an inn that was once the local mill. The parish church has an unusual open-sided bell-tower and the east end is graced by splendid Perpendicular windows. The church interior has many interesting monuments but the most famous are those of members of the Fettiplace family. Two three-level wall monuments show six male members of the family. They are all lying on their right sides and looking outwards into the church rather than piously upwards. The churchyard contains a number of traditional table tombs as well as the graves of Unity, Diana, Pamela and Nancy Mitford. The Mitfords lived at nearby Asthall and later at Swinbrook House which was built by their father, Lord Redesdale. An account of life at Swinbrook can be found in Jessica Mitford's book *Hons and Rebels*. Both Asthall and Swinbrook House are within easy walking distance of the village.

Widford

The hamlet of Widford lies close to neighbouring Swinbrook. Widford was a substantial village in medieval times but now few houses remain. Characteristic crop-marks of former buildings can be seen in the surrounding fields. The ancient church of St Oswald sits on a rise above the river and was built over a Roman tessellated pavement. The church interior features a number of wall paintings dating from the mid-14th century. The painting of St Christopher is badly defaced and worn so that only his staff is clearly visible. There is a better preserved painting of kings and ghosts which can be seen in the chancel.

Great Barrington

Great Barrington began its life as an estate village and much of it remains so today. A great deal of the stone that makes the Cotswolds so distinctive was quarried in the area surrounding this village. Barrington Park was originally the seat of the Bray family but it became the property of Earl Talbot, Lord Chancellor in the reign of George II. The house was rebuilt in the Palladian style in 1738.

Little Barrington

The sloping, hollowed-out village green at Little Barrington is on the site of a quarry that supplied much of the Cotswolds with its distinctive stone. The village also produced one of the most famous stonemasons of the 17th century, Thomas Strong, who worked with Sir Christopher Wren on St Paul's and other London churches.

Taynton

This compact Oxfordshire village stands on the border between Gloucestershire and Oxfordshire. Confusingly there is also a Taynton in Gloucestershire. Taynton stone, quarried nearby, was highly prized during the Middle Ages and early modern period and can be found in local buildings, Oxford colleges and many of Sir Christopher Wren's London churches. Stone from the Taynton quarries would have been hauled overland to the river Thames at Radcot bridge or Lechlade. From these places it would have continued its journey by barge. One contemporary account describes a load of stone being pulled by a team of 21 horses. Taynton church dates from 1450 and is unusual in being in the Decorated style rather than Perpendicular. Given the importance of stone to Tayton's parishioners it is not surprising to find some excellent stone carving in the church. The font consists of an octagonal bowl with kneeling angels at each corner and figures of beasts, the Evangelists and a mermaid in between. There are also vividly carved corbel heads in the nave and north transept which show off the elaborate headwear of the late medieval period. Two carved figures in the north transept are thought to be King Henry VI and the Abbot of Tewkesbury.

Windrush

Windrush is named after the river on which it stands and has a small tree-lined green next to an attractive church. Windrush is a former quarrying village and possesses many fine houses built from local stone. A few of the houses date from the 17th century and one is dated 1668. St Peter's church is of Norman origin and has been Windrush's parish church since 1586. The south doorway is elaborately carved with menacing looking beaked heads which are mixed with the heads of other fantastical beasts. In the churchyard there is a finely decorated wool bale tomb, which represents the source of the deceased's wealth in the form of corded bales of wool. South of the village is the Iron Age hill fort of Windrush Camp.

Bledington

Bledington is in the Evenlode valley and is built around a wide village green. The village church is located to the south of the green and there is a charming row of cottages overlooking the churchyard. The church was refurbished in the 15th century out of profits from the wool trade. As well as a very old doorway with its original door, the interior features several 15th century Perpendicular windows containing stained glass believed to be the work of John Pruddle, the master craftsman who produced the windows of Beauchamp chapel in Warwick.

Little and Wyck Rissington

Little Rissington and Wyck Rissington are small villages to the east of Bourton-on-the-Water. Each has its own church. Perhaps the most famous of the villages is Little Rissington. The RAF flying school was located just outside the village in the Second World War and memorials in St Peter's churchyard commemorate the many pilots who died. There is also a stained-glass memorial to the pilots in the church itself. After the war RAF Little Rissington served as the headquarters of the Red Arrows aerial display team. The village has a number of fine houses and some picturesque wells. Wyck Rissington's greatest claim to fame is the fact that the composer Gustav Holst was given his first professional position as an organist at the church of St Lawrence. One of the more eccentric vicars at the church, Canon Henry Cheaves, built a maze between the rectory and the church to symbolise the Christian path through life. The maze has been removed but the canon's memorial in the church records its shape. Also worth seeking out in the churchyard here is the well-tended grave of a traveller, James Loveridge, whose life ended in the village.

Sherborne

During the Middle Ages Sherborne's plentiful water supply made it an ideal centre for sheep-shearing. In fact, at that time there was little else in Sherborne apart from sheep and the Abbot of Winchcombe's summer palace. With the Dissolution of the Monasteries the land passed to the Dutton family and by 1651 Sherborne House had been built. The present Sherborne grew up as an estate village for Sherborne House. The Dutton family remained in residence there until the 1980s when the estate was bequeathed to the National Trust. Sherborne House, which was extensively rebuilt in the 19th century, is now divided into luxury flats and the rest of the estate is dedicated to improved access to the land and nature conservation. Sherborne church is near the park and has a medieval tower and spire; it is chiefly interesting for its many monuments and memorials to the Dutton family.

Bourton-on-the-Water

Five ornamental bridges span the river Windrush in Bourton-on-the-Water giving it a unique appeal and the nickname of the "Venice of the Cotswolds". Moving downstream, the five bridges are: Bourton Bridge built in 1806 and widened in 1959; Mill Bridge (also known as Broad Bridge) built in 1654 on the site of a former ford; High Bridge, a footbridge built in 1756; New Bridge (or Moore Bridge) built in 1911 to traverse another ford; and Coronation Bridge, built in 1953 to replace an 18th century wooden bridge. During the summer, a game of football is attempted between two of the bridges. The goalposts are set in the river and teams play using a standard football. The aim of the game is to score as many goals as possible but the general effect is to get everyone else as wet as possible. Bourton-on-the-Water is served by the parish church of St Lawrence. The only visible part of the old church is the chancel, built in 1328 by Walter de Burhton. In 1784 the Norman church was largely replaced with today's neo-Classical style building with its thick tower housing a clock and bells. Further additions were made in the 1870s when the present nave was constructed. The nave roof is a fine example of a king-post roof.

Other attractions in this popular village include: the Dragonfly Maze with over a quarter of a mile of pathways and an attractive pavilion at its centre; Birdland, a bird sanctuary that includes a small colony of penguins; the Cotswold Motor Museum; and the Model Village which is a ninth scale replica of the village. The model Bourton-on-the-Water contains a model of the model village whilst Bourton-on-the-Water itself also contains a model railway exhibition and Miniature World.

On a larger scale visitors can see collections of pottery at the studio in Clapton Row and an exhibition of village life housed in an 18th century water mill. On the edge of the village is a series of flooded gravel pits which have been established as a nature reserve with a wide variety of bird life.

Eastleach Martin and Eastleach Turville

The two villages at Eastleach, Turville and Martin, face each other across the river Leach. The two villages once belonged to different manors and therefore have their own manor houses and churches. Eastleach Martin has the larger of the churches and its 14th century north transept is graced with three Decorated-style windows. Eastleach Turville's church has a 14th century saddleback tower and a Norman tympanum. The two churches are 200 yards apart and the villages are connected by two bridges. One bridge carries the road but the other is an unusual construction of large flat stones. This footbridge is known as Keble's Bridge and commemorates the Keble family who were lords of the manor of Eastleach Turville in the 16th century. The most famous member of the Keble family was John who founded the Oxford Movement and after whom Keble College Oxford is named. The peaceful aspect of today's villages makes it difficult to imagine that there were once anti-machinery riots here. By the 19th century wool production had largely been replaced by corn growing and by the 1830s the introduction of threshing machines began to put people out of work. Several machines were destroyed by desperate labourers in the area resulting in imprisonment and transportation for those involved.

Southrop

Southrop is a pleasant village on the river Leach which used to be owned by Wadham College Oxford. The village's most famous inhabitant was John Keble, the founder of the Oxford Movement for the reform of the Church of England. Keble was working as a curate in Southrop when he formulated the movement's basic principles with three friends. The church of St Peter is a plain and simple building with a long and varied history. The Norman main part dates from around 1100 whilst the 13th century chancel is in Early English style. The most impressive feature of the church is the carved Norman font; each of its panels represents a virtue triumphing over a vice.

Fairford

The jewel in Fairford's crown is the church of St Mary. Constructed in the late Perpendicular style it celebrates the wealth and power of the Tame family who built it out of profits from the wool industry. St Mary's stained-glass windows survived 17th century Puritan purges and are a particularly fine example of late medieval work. Other notable buildings in Fairford include an early 18th century free school decorated with plaques to esteemed teachers, the 17th century Bull Hotel, Fairford mill and the oxpen.

PART SIX

AROUND STROUD

🌿

THE LONG HISTORY OF HUMAN HABITATION in the Cotswolds has left its mark on the landscape. Iron Age forts were often sited on hills for ease of defence, Roman roads carved the area up with straight lines to facilitate military transport and the growth of sheep-farming in the Middle Ages led to the opening up of large fields. Later still canals, railways and modern roads provided new routes through the area. Probably the most characteristic boundary marker in the Cotswolds is the drystone wall. Built with great skill without any binding materials, these massive dividers criss-cross the Cotswolds and are a permanent reminder of the efforts of the countless unknown craftsmen who toiled to build them.

TIMELESS LANDSCAPE
Life in the hidden village of Slad (above) in the 1920s was made famous by Laurie Lee who immortalised the valley in his novel *Cider with Rosie*. Sunset on a crisp winter's day over Cam Long Down (right)

Stroud

Five valleys come together at Stroud making it a natural centre for trade and transport. In the Middle Ages Stroud quickly established itself as a centre of the cloth industry and at the height of its prosperity there were 150 cloth mills in and around the town. Stroud was particularly famous for manufacturing the cloth used in military uniforms. The centre of Stroud reflects its role as a market town with its many narrow streets, its Tudor town hall and the area known as the Shambles which catered for butchers. The neo-Classical Subscription Rooms (built by public subscription in the 19th century) are now a venue for concerts and exhibitions.

Stroud today

The decline of the wool trade did not dampen Stroud's spirits overmuch and the area increasingly became a centre for light industry in the late 19th and early 20th centuries. Fortunately, industrial growth has not seriously diminished the town's charm and modern Stroud emphasises its relaxed atmosphere and alternative lifestyles. Stroud now plays host to lively music and dance festivals and to a flourishing arts scene. Pavement cafés and small art galleries are common. The five valleys that meet at Stroud provide easy access to different parts of the Cotswolds and so make the town a good starting point for visitors exploring the area.

Minchinhampton

This attractive village, centred on its High Street and old Market Square, was once one of the most important cloth towns in the Cotswolds. Minchinhampton was not easily accessible by road and this meant that it retained more of its old-fashioned charm than many similar towns. The square is dominated by the 17th century Market House which is supported on sturdy stone pillars. Nearby is a post office which is housed in a Queen Anne building. Parts of the church date from the 12th century but the top of the spire had to be removed to prevent collapse in 1863. The truncated stub has been finished with an unusual "coronet". Of particular interest in the interior is the 14th century south transept which contains a varied collection of tomb recesses and effigies in the Decorated style.

Minchinhampton Common

The 600-acre Minchinhampton Common was granted to the people of the village in the 16th century; to encourage the settlement of skilled people a weaver was allowed to enclose land on it and build a cottage. The common is now owned and managed by the National Trust and its elevated location makes it a popular destination for ramblers. As well as being a popular recreation area the common contains several important archaeological sites. The most visible and extensive Iron Age remains slightly pre-date the Roman conquest and indicate that the area was a strategic location for the Dobunni tribe. Known as the Bulwarks these large defensive earthworks are over a mile long. Nearby is Amberley Camp which is a hill fort enclosing around 50 acres. There are also many round and long barrows in the area.

Amberley

Amberley is located on the western edge of Minchinhampton Common. The village commands splendid views over the steep valley of the Nailsworth stream. The village today is a scattered settlement that has taken various guises since the Middle Ages. The original woodlands in the area gave way to sheep-farming during that period. Most of the older buildings in the area are former weaver's cottages. The parish church of the Holy Trinity at Amberley was not erected until 1837.

Avening

The medieval village of Avening grew up around the Norman church of the Holy Rood. Dating from 1080 and occupying the site of an earlier Saxon church, Holy Rood has several points of interest for those who venture inside. The south transept houses a small museum that has models of the church at various periods of its life as well as a Saxon skeleton and some wild boar tusks. One of the monuments is dedicated to a former pirate. Avening also boasts a number of substantial buildings built out of the profits of the wool trade. Local streams once provided power for a mill and water for cloth processing. Just above the village are three burial chambers excavated from a nearby long barrow in 1806.

Nailsworth

Nailsworth is about three miles south of Stroud in one of that town's five valleys. Nailsworth is itself at the meeting place of three valleys which branch off towards Avening, Horsley and Stroud. Access to the village was quite difficult in the Middle Ages and would have mainly been via packhorse. The modern A46 now causes transport problems of a different sort as it runs through the centre of Nailsworth. The village's plentiful water supply enabled the construction of large woollen mills and one of them, Egypt Mill, has now been restored with its water wheels and most of its gearing still intact. The building now operates as a restaurant. The nearby Ruskin mill has become an arts and crafts centre and also has a working water wheel. At the centre of the town there is a fine mid-20th century clock tower and many of the steep and narrow streets contain substantial buildings from earlier periods; for

instance a fine 17th century Quaker Meeting House. About two miles north-west of Nailsworth is Woodchester Park. This delightful wooded valley which runs towards Nympsfield has numerous springs along its length and is a popular choice for walkers in the area. Other walks head south towards Chavenage and Beverstone.

111

Uley

Uley is a large village situated in a wooded valley on the Cotswold escarpment. It was a cloth-producing centre and was formerly renowned for its blue cloth; several substantial 18th century houses in the village owe their existence to the wool trade. Now the village has its own brewery and also a well-designed Victorian church. Near Uley, at West Hill, there are the remains of a Roman temple built on top of an earlier prehistoric shrine.

Nympsfield

Nympsfield is a small village at the head of a valley near the Cotswold edge which developed along the route of a former Roman road from Cirencester to Arlingham. The village grew up as a busy stopping place on a coaching route and in its heyday there were five inns in the village catering for passing trade. Nympsfield long barrow has been extensively excavated and is open to the sky allowing visitors to see the interior of this ancient burial place.

Owlpen

The Owlpen Manor estate includes the manor itself, a 19th century church, a small 18th century mill and a number of cottages nearby. With an adult population of around 35 the parish of Owlpen is the smallest in Gloucestershire. The manor house dates from 1450 to 1616 and it was extensively restored in 1926 after almost a hundred years of neglect and dereliction. It features a Tudor Great Hall, a Jacobean Solar, an early Georgian Little Parlour and a Great Chamber. The latter room contains unique painted cloth wall-hangings showing biblical scenes from the life of Joseph and his brothers. Owlpen Manor is reputedly haunted by Margaret of Anjou, the queen consort of Henry VI. She is said to appear as a lady in beautiful clothes drifting through the rooms of the house. Margaret stayed at Owlpen Manor in 1471 before the Battle of Tewkesbury, which her faction lost. She was then imprisoned and her son was killed. The restoration of Owlpen was undertaken by Norman Jewson who bought the house in the 1920s but unfortunately could not afford to live in it thereafter. The interior of the church has a number of fine paintings and some impressive mosaics.

Woodchester

Woodchester lies in the valley of the Nailsworth stream two miles south of Stroud and is divided into North and South Woodchester. To the south-west of the village is Woodchester Park which contains the ruins of a large 19th century mansion. The building was instigated by William Leigh, a wealthy merchant, who purchased the park in 1846. Leigh wanted to live in a Gothic revival mansion and approached several architects including Pugin to plan his new home. Construction began in 1858 and continued until 1870 but when William Leigh died in 1873 all work stopped. Some parts of the never-completed house were occupied by Leigh's family and at various times it served as a mental health hospital and a teacher-training college. Shortly after the Second World War the house was abandoned but fortunately it never completely fell into ruins. The Woodchester Mansion Trust took over the building in 1992 and it is now open to the public. The Trust also provides training courses on stone conservation and other traditional crafts.

Woodchester history

The village of Woodchester grew up as a processing centre for the wool industry and between 1750 and 1820 there were 10 mills in the Woodchester area. The plentiful supplies of water in the valley provided power for the mills as well as for fulling and dyeing. A napping machine was invented at Southfields Mill and opposite Frogmarsh Mill is the unique 16th century Teasel Tower. Its name derives from the fact that it was used to store the teasels (dried prickly plant heads) used to raise the nap on cloth. Also in Woodchester are the remains of a large Roman villa. Eighteenth century excavations in St Mary's churchyard revealed a beautiful mosaic pavement showing the Orpheus story. It is now covered up to protect it but a replica has been made and may be seen on display at Prinknash.

Cam Long Down

A popular site for walkers and sightseers, Cam Long Down is linked to the main Cotswold escarpment via a saddle to Cam Peak. The top of Cam Long Down forms a narrow plateau which is famous for its wild flowers. The views from the top extend over the river Severn, the Forest of Dean and the curve of the Cotswold escarpment itself. To the south-west can be seen the town of Dursley and to the south the wooded top of Downham Hill, another outlying peak, which is known locally as Smallpox Hill. To the south stands the Tyndale Monument, dedicated to William Tyndale, translator of the New Testament into English.

Coaley Peak

Coaley Peak picnic site consists of 12 acres of grassland on the edge of the Cotswold escarpment. It was purchased by Gloucestershire County Council in 1972 for public recreation and at that time was mostly arable land; today wildflowers and grasses flourish. The site commands wide-ranging views across the Severn Vale and the Forest of Dean and is bordered to the south by the Frocester Hill nature reserve and to the north-east by Stanley woods. Woodchester Park, a beautiful valley containing a "lost" garden and a chain of five lakes, owned by the National Trust, lies to the east. At the centre of the site is the Nympsfield long barrow, a Neolithic burial chamber dating back to about 2900BC. It was excavated in 1937 and 1974 and the remains of at least 16 skeletons were recovered.

Bowbridge from Rodborough

The village of Rodborough is on the edge of Stroud and occupies the end of a spur of land which rises to over 600ft (183m). Rodborough church has a stained glass window depicting Thomas the Tank Engine in memory of the Reverend Wilbert Awdry who lived in the village from 1965 onwards. Rodborough is also home to Winstone's ice cream factory. Above the village is Rodborough Common; the ancient road from London to Stroud used to run across here and provided the village with carriage trade. The common was acquired by the National Trust in 1937 and now provides a stretch of open countryside for mainly recreational purposes. A prominent landmark on the common is an inhabited folly called Rodborough Fort. It was built around 1764 by George Hawker, presumably as a rural retreat, and achieved its present castellated Gothic form in 1868 when it was extensively rebuilt. Bowbridge is located below Rodborough on the river Frome and was a main crossing point en route from Stroud to the east. Bowbridge fulling mill operated there from 1608 until 1927 with a lock for the Thames and Severn canal being added in 1789.

Selsley

Selsley is a small village which occupies the eastern and western edge of a Cotswold spur. The church at Selsley was paid for by a wealthy mill owner in the 19th century and is in the French-Gothic style. It is notable for its stained glass which was donated by leading pre-Raphaelites such as Rossetti, Morris, Ford Madox Brown and Burne-Jones. Running through the village is Water Lane, a prehistoric track that in places has ten feet high banks. To the south-west of the village is Selsley Common, a 160-acre open expanse used for recreation and occasional cattle grazing. It offers superb views to the west over the Severn valley.

Slad

Slad is a small village that stretches out along the side of a valley north-east of Stroud. It was the childhood home of the author Laurie Lee. Life in the village in the 1920s is brilliantly evoked in Laurie Lee's autobiography *Cider With Rosie* but the present village has not let literary fame go to its head. It remains remarkably unspoiled and it is still possible to gain a sense of the quiet pre-motor car village described by Laurie Lee in the 1920s. Lee's "local", The Wool Pack inn, mentioned in the book, is still trading. The earliest references to Slad come from 1353 when a bridge was built there to cross the Slad Brook, but the oldest building is probably Steanbridge House, an early 17th century gabled clothier's house. Some weavers' cottages also date from this period but the church of the Holy Trinity and the village school were built in the 1830s. Laurie Lee is buried in the graveyard of the church.

Bisley

The many fine houses in and around Bisley are a testament to the wealth created by the cloth trade in the 18th century. At one end of the village are five water chutes known locally as "The Wells"; they were restored to commemorate the Reverend Thomas Keble, brother of John, who was rector of Bisley for nearly 50 years. As was common in many Cotswold communities the village has a small 19th century two-person lock-up; with its ogee-gables Bisley's is a particularly fine example.

Miserden

Most of the buildings in Miserden are 19th and 20th century in origin but the village has had a long history of growth, decay and renewal. Near to the village are the earthworks of a motte and bailey castle which was erected shortly after the Norman Conquest. The name Miserden is a corruption of the name of the family, la Musarder, that held the manor from the 12th century onwards. Among the surviving 17th century houses are the rectory, Lampacre cottage and a pair of cottages, one of which used to be the blacksmith's. The two-storey dower house dates from the 18th century and had an east wing added in the 1860s by Sir John Rolt; Sir John also rebuilt other parts of the village. The church has late Saxon origins although it was extensively restored in the 1880s. The war memorial was designed by Sir Edwin Lutyens who also carried out work at Misarden Park, a large Elizabethan mansion with exquisite gardens just to the east of the village. A comparatively recent feature is a small octagonal shelter built around a large sycamore tree.

Caudle Green

This is a delightful hamlet set in the deeply incised valley of the upper reaches of the river Frome, a mile north-east of Miserden, its larger neighbour. The farmhouse facing the village green is a rectangular mid 18th century building of five bays in ashlar stonework and there are a number of traditional cottages built in the Cotswold vernacular. Walks on the local footpaths give visitors the impression of being completely cut off from the modern world.

Cranham

Built at the head of a valley, Cranham enjoys excellent views plus access to a large common to the south and extensive beech woods to the north. The parish church of St James the Great is in the south-western part of the village and dominates the surrounding countryside. It was built largely in the 15th century when the area prospered as a result of sheep-rearing. This is commemorated on the church itself by two pairs of sheep-shears carved onto the second stage of the church tower. Inside the church there is an early 16th century rood screen and a monument to Obadiah Done who was rector to the parish for 57 years. The composer Gustav Holst lived briefly in Cranham and whilst there he wrote what is probably the best-known tune for Christina Rossetti's Christmas carol *In the Bleak Midwinter*. The tune is called *Cranham* and the house where he stayed is now called Midwinter Cottage. The Cotswold Way long-distance footpath runs near to Cranham.

Sheepscombe

As its name suggests, Sheepscombe is situated in a narrow secluded valley tucked into the folded landscape east of Painswick. It was originally the site of a deer park and hunting ground but in the 17th century it benefited from the growth of the textile industry. Many of the houses in the village date from this period of industrial expansion. Woollen mills were also introduced but decline followed in the late 18th and early 19th centuries; the last mill closed in 1839. The village church of St John the Apostle was built in 1820 and a school was opened in 1822; the school was later modernised in 1882. To the east of Sheepscombe is Workman's Wood, a site of special scientific interest which is one of only three sites in Britain where the rare plant Red Helleborine is found.

Painswick

The stream below Painswick once provided power for its woollen mills whilst its crystal clear water made the village an important centre for cloth dyeing. Many of the houses in the village date from the 17th and 18th centuries and once belonged to wealthy wool merchants. At the centre of the village is a fine church which combines sections from the 15th century with an elegant 17th century tower. Surrounding the church are well-tended colonnades of yew trees which have been in place since 1792. Local legend has it that there are only 99 trees as the devil always kills the hundredth. Each year in September the Painswick Clipping Ceremony is held. This has nothing to do with keeping the yews in check but takes its name from the Old English word *clyppan* meaning to embrace. Groups of children form a circle around the church then approach and retreat from it three times whilst singing a hymn. A cake containing a porcelain dog, known as "puppy dog pie" was traditionally baked on this day.

Haresfield and Harescombe

Haresfield Hill lies on the edge of the Cotswold escarpment, three miles north-west of Stroud. The Cotswold Way national trail runs along the escarpment. The 429 acre Haresfield estate, made up of beech woodland and open grassland, and which includes Haresfield Beacon, is owned by the National Trust. Haresfield Beacon is the site of a Romano-British hill fort and has wonderful views across the Severn Vale, including the village from which it takes its name.

The nearby hamlet of Harescombe consists of a scattering of farms and cottages with the beautifully situated church of St John the Baptist at the foot of the rising hills.

Edge

A fine example of Cotswold literalism, the village of Edge is on the edge of the escarpment. It commands fine views westwards over the Severn Vale and eastwards towards Painswick. Edge was a fashionable place for picnics and outings even in the 19th century and its small Victorian church was built at the behest of the owner of nearby Harescombe Grange. The church is unremarkable but the churchyard is carpeted with snowdrops in the spring. There are several Roman sites nearby and the ghost of a Roman centurion is said to roam the area. Beatrix Potter was a frequent visitor to Harescombe Grange and whilst staying there she had the idea for *The Tailor of Gloucester*. Another literary connection is provided by the large house know as Hilles. It was built by Detmar Blow, a former mayor of Painswick, who was a friend of William Morris. Rudyard Kipling also spent several holidays at the house.